WUTHERII A WORKSI

Jane O'Neill
Formerly Head of English
Long Road Sixth Form College
Cambridge

Literary Images Limited

1

First published in the UK in 1992 by
Literary Images Limited
Braceborough
Lincolnshire PE9 4NT

Reprinted 1996

British Library Cataloguing in Publication Data
A catalogue record for this book is available from The British Library

© Literary Images Limited 1992
ISBN 1 874274 002

All rights reserved. No part of this publication may be reproduced, stored in a retrieval system or transmitted in any form or by any means, electronic, mechanical, photocopying, recording or otherwise, without prior permission in writing from Literary Images Limited.

Design by Ravelin Limited, Lincolnshire
Typeset by Vitaset, Paddock Wood, Kent
Printed in Great Britain by Robendene Ltd

2

Contents

Introduction

This 'study guide' to *Wuthering Heights* aims at drawing attention to the main elements or aspects of the novel which any serious reader must address, e.g. the main 'themes', imagery – so important in this novel, where the landscape and isolation of the Yorkshire moors play a major part – the role of narrator, structure and style. This Guide is not intended to present a particular critical viewpoint of *Wuthering Heights*, for which the reader should turn to the many critical studies available.

By asking very specific questions and demanding close textual reference in support of answers, the Worksheet for Students directs the reader to look closely at the text. The Worksheet Guide provides suggested interpretations, where appropriate or necessary, and specific textual reference for the questions asked on the student sheet (to enable readers to find these references and quotations easily, page numbers to the Penguin edition of the novel are given. Readers should note that, in order to distinguish between the two Catherines of the novel, the older one is referred to by her full name, the younger is always called 'Cathy').

Where the punctuation in quotations differs from that of the Penguin edition, the source used is the Norton (Third) Critical Edition. In the absence of an extant manuscript of *Wuthering Heights*, editors have either adopted Charlotte's version of the text, as it appeared in the second edition of the novel, or they have used both the first and second editions as sources for their own. In this spirit, both the Norton and Penguin editions have been used here.

Teachers should find this Guide useful in preparing the text for teaching, in actually working through the novel with a class, and in revision. Students themselves find it a very useful self-help tool, both in studying the novel and in revising for examinations. Space has been left at the end of each section for the reader's own notes. The author has used these textually-based worksheets very successfully with A level students for a number of years.

Although this 'study guide' should prove helpful to both students and teachers, it is not intended only for them. The detailed Guide, providing specific textual references, should be useful to all those who want help with approaching a text in greater critical depth.

Jane O'Neill

PHYSICAL CHARACTERISTICS OF
WUTHERING HEIGHTS (Q.1).

The physical description of the position of the house and the house itself all convey the impression of a lonely, socially isolated place, exposed to the elements: the wind and storm. The house itself is presented as a stronghold, "defended" against the elements and, indeed, against all comers. It is uncared for – "crumbling griffins" – and has a Gothic strangeness about it – "grotesque carving lavished" over the front and main door; but these also suggest a past grandeur and importance. Its age and the name above the door reinforce this, and they also kindle our curiosity: who was Hareton Earnshaw?

It is worth noting here that the strangeness and suspense created in the opening pages of *WUTHERING HEIGHTS* are further reinforced by other Gothic elements in the novel, particularly the supernatural. In the first seven chapters, for instance, we find mentioned *'fairy'* (**pp.55 and 56**), *'changeling'* (**p.69**), *'witch'* and *'witches'* (**pp.57 and 89**), *'spectres'* and *'spectre'* (**pp.61 and 70**), *'ghosts'* (**p.68**) and *'goblins'* (**p.68**). And the supernatural continues to play a major role throughout the novel, most notably perhaps in the scene where Heathcliff describes sensing Catherine's presence on the earth beside him as he tries to open her coffin on the night of her burial (**p.320**), and finally, of course, in the last chapter of the novel, when the little boy "crying terribly" tells Lockwood that he cannot pass "Heathcliff and a woman, yonder" and "neither the sheep nor he would go on." (**p.366**).

The description of the interior of the house is detailed and precise. There is a strange mixture of lack of life in the absence of cooking and "the glitter" of copper and tin on the one hand and yet the pewter and silver reflect both light and heat, and the colours repeat this mixture: black and liver-coloured, white and green. The "villainous old guns" and horse-pistols above the chimney suggest the violence we are going to associate with Wuthering Heights as we learn to know it better.

SUGGESTED REFERENCES:

Isolated: "In all England, I do not believe that I could have fixed on a situation so completely removed from the stir of society. A perfect misanthropist's heaven . . ." (**p.45**).

Exposed to the elements: "one may guess the power of the north wind, blowing over the edge, by the excessive slant of a few stunted firs at the end of the house; and by a range of gaunt thorns all stretching their limbs one way, as if craving alms of the sun." (**p.46**).

Strong: "Happily, the architect had foresight to build it strong: the narrow windows are deeply set in the wall, and the corners defended with large jutting stones." (**p.46**).

'Gothic', with suggestions of past grandeur: There is "grotesque carving lavished over the front, and especially about the principal door, above which, among a wilderness of crumbling griffins and shameless little boys, I detected the date '1500' and the name 'Hareton Earnshaw'." (**p.46**).

Its interior is both light and dark, colourful and gloomy: There are "no signs of roasting, boiling or baking about the huge fire-place, nor any glitter of copper saucepans and tin cullenders on the walls", but "One end, indeed, reflected splendidly both light and heat, from ranks of immense pewter dishes, interspersed with silver jugs and tankards, towering row after row." Above the chimney are "three gaudily painted cannisters"; the floor is of "smooth, white stone"; the chairs are green or black; and the bitch liver-coloured. (**pp.46, 47**).

Violent: The villainous guns and horse-pistols (**p.47**).

Notes:

ATMOSPHERE (Q.2).

a) "Heathcliff stood near the entrance, in his shirt and trousers, with a candle dripping over his fingers, and his face as white as the wall behind him. The first creak of the oak startled him like an electric shock: the light leaped from his hold to a distance of some feet, and his agitation was so extreme that he could hardly pick it up." (**p.68**).

In this passage the sense of Heathcliff's 'agitation' is conveyed in several ways: in his physical description – the colour of his face and the way he has neglected to stop the candle grease from dripping over his hands. Words like "creak", "startled", "shock", "leaped" all suggest his "extreme" disquiet. The two similes – "white as the wall" and "like an electric shock" – reinforce the picture.

b) "We deferred our excursion till the afternoon; a golden afternoon of August – every breath from the hills so full of life, that it seemed whoever respired it, though dying, might revive.

Catherine's face was just like the landscape – shadows and sunshine flitting over it, in rapid succession; but the shadows rested longer and the sunshine was more transient, and her poor little heart reproached itself for even that passing forgetfulness of its cares." (**pp.297, 298**).

The description of the afternoon is of a life-giving, "golden" one, but the appearance is deceptive. Again, we have a simile – this time used to compare Catherine's face to the landscape. We are told that "shadows and sunshine flitted over it" but that the shadows rested longer than the sunshine. Words like "rapid", "flitted", "transient" convey the change of mood; and the emphasis on shadows and the reference to her "poor little" heart and "cares" suggest the prevailing sadness.

c) "He was leaning against the ledge of an open lattice, but not looking out; his face was turned to the interior gloom. The fire had smouldered to ashes; the room was filled with the damp, mild air of the cloudy evening, and so still, that not only the murmur of the beck down Gimmerton was distinguishable, but its ripples and its gurgling over the pebbles, or through the large stones which it could not cover."(**p.359**).

Here Heathcliff's mood is conveyed by the images: the window is open, but he is not looking outwards; the fire – the centre of life – is dead; the water images are here in the damp cloudy evening and in the beck – water rippling over pebbles and "through the large stones which it could not cover". The images are still there on the moors today. All is still, so still that the natural world alone speaks. He is approaching death, when he will be absorbed into the elements.

Notes:

THE ELEMENTS (Q.3).

The elemental images are probably the most prevalent and the most important in the novel. The world which Emily Brontë has created is one of elemental passion, and it is through these images that she conveys that passion. We can see how important a part the landscape (and weather) of the Yorkshire moors plays in creating the atmosphere and conveying the main 'themes' of *Wuthering Heights*, as well as contributing to the interpretation of character.

Earth:

The moors are the setting for the novel – the place where Catherine and Heathcliff are at home, even in death. They are a place which represents for them freedom – escape from the tyranny of Hindley – and the place of which Catherine dreams (her "heaven"). And the earth is the place of their final union, for which both Catherine and Heathcliff long. Many of the references to earth in the novel are associated with death and graves. Catherine's love for Heathcliff, she tells Nelly, "resembles the eternal rocks beneath."

SUGGESTED REFERENCES:

a) "On that bleak hill-top the earth was hard with a black frost, and the air made me shiver through every limb." (**p.51**).

In this passage, Emily Brontë is still creating or setting the scene. It heralds Lockwood's second visit to Wuthering Heights and establishes, once again, its hostility to visitors in her use of adjectives and verbs – "bleak", "black" and the air made him "shiver".

b) ". . . heaven did not seem to be my home; and I broke my heart with weeping to come back to earth; and the angels were so angry that they flung me out, into the middle of the heath on the top of Wuthering Heights, where I woke sobbing for joy." (**pp.120, 121**).

Catherine belongs to the moors and to Heathcliff, not, significantly, to heaven, as seen through conventional Christian eyes. Here, she is explaining to Nelly why she should not marry Edgar, who is identified in the novel with traditional Christian values (we see him coming from church, for example). Heathcliff, on the other hand, is associated in the novel with anti-Christian forces – Satan, the Devil, Hell – and with the forces of nature: the moors, the wind, rain and snow.

c) "The place of Catherine's interment, to the surprise of the villagers, was neither in the chapel, under the carved monument of the Lintons, nor yet by the tombs of her own relations, outside. It was dug on a green slope in a corner of the kirkyard, where the wall is so low that heath and bilberry plants have climbed over it from the moor; and peat almost buries it." (**p.205**).

Catherine's grave is as close to the moor, to which she belongs, as it can be and still remain within consecrated ground. Emily Brontë specifically tells us that she is not buried in the chapel, nor with either Linton's family or her own. She does not belong with any of those, but to the wild, natural forces which are her and Heathcliff's true element. Here we see that the plants and the peat of the moors have invaded the churchyard to claim their own.

d) "I sought, and soon discovered, the three head-stones on the slope next the moor – the middle one, grey, and half buried in heath – Edgar Linton's only harmonized by the turf and moss, creeping up its foot – Heathcliff's still bare.

I lingered round them, under that benign sky; watched the moths fluttering among the heath and hare-bells; listened to the soft wind breathing through the grass; and wondered how anyone could ever imagine unquiet slumbers, for the sleepers in that quiet earth." (**p.367**).

In this final paragraph of the novel, only Edgar's grave is "harmonized". Catherine's is 'half buried in heath', Heathcliff's too recent to be anything but bare. (Are we left to imagine it eventually covered in the same way as Catherine's?) Peace has, at last, descended on and enveloped this passionate, violent world: the sky is "benign", the moths "flutter" (note the soft sounds), and the wind is "soft"; the "sleepers" "slumber" in the "quiet" earth.

Notes:

Air:

The wind and air are bearers of the storm in *Wuthering Heights*: in them is centred much of the violence and the passion that we find in the novel. But air also suggests movement and life.

SUGGESTED REFERENCES:

a) Lockwood "heard distinctly the gusty wind, and the driving of the snow" and his dreams are suggested by the branch of a fir tree that "rattled its dry cones against the panes." (**p.66**).

Here we see clearly the elements as bearers of the storm and fitting metaphorical vehicles for the primitive passions unleashed. (Compare *King Lear*).

b) ". . . the snow and wind whirled wildly through, even reaching my station, and blowing out the light." (**p.70**).

Here we see the violence of the elements which accompany the "anguish" of Heathcliff, as he calls to the "spectre" of Catherine: "He got onto the bed, and wrenched open the lattice, bursting, as he pulled at it, into an uncontrollable passion of tears." The 'uncontrolled' elements reflect his own lack of emotional control.

c) "I declined joining their breakfast, and, at the first gleam of dawn, took an opportunity of escaping into the free air, now clear and still, and cold as impalpable ice." (**p.72**).

Although Lockwood has escaped from Wuthering Heights after his unnerving night there, he still emerges into a hostile environment to which he does not naturally belong: the air is "cold as impalpable ice".

d) Cathy's idea of heaven is "rocking in a rustling green tree, with a west wind blowing, and bright, white clouds flitting rapidly above . . . [and] close by, great swells of long grass undulating in waves to the breeze." (**p.280**).

Cathy and Linton have come "near quarrelling" over their differing ideas of "heaven's happiness". Linton's is of stillness and cloudless skies; Cathy's is of movement – "rocking", "rustling", "blowing", "flitting", "undulating" all convey to us her vitality and, of course, her unsuitability as a partner for Linton. These images of air are the vehicles for expressing her essential nature. It is interesting to remember that Emily Brontë also used elemental images to convey the difference between Cathy's mother and Edgar: "Whatever our souls are made of, his [Heathcliff's] and mine are the same, and Linton's is as different as a moonbeam from lightning or frost from fire." (**p.121**).

e) "I was on the point of attaining my object, when it seemed that I heard a sigh from someone above, close at the edge of the grave, and bending down . . . There was another sigh, close at my ear. I appeared to feel the warm breath of it displacing the sleet-laden wind. I knew no living thing in flesh and blood was by . . ." (**p.320**).

We see here how Emily Brontë conveys the insubstantiality of Catherine's ghost through the image of air: She is a "sigh", a "warm breath", which replaces the "sleet-laden wind". Her physical body cannot withstand "the air", as the sexton warns Heathcliff when he opens the coffin eighteen years later (**p.319**); but her spirit can wander at will amongst the elements, ". . . as certainly as you perceive the approach to some substantial body in the dark, though it cannot be discerned, so certainly I felt that Cathy was there, not under me, but on the earth." (**pp.320, 321**).

Notes:

Fire:

Fire is traditionally associated with life and light as well as with heat. In *Wuthering Heights* it is usually the centre of life in the room, but it is also associated with extreme emotion, used metaphorically in the description of character.

SUGGESTED REFERENCES:

a) "After . . . making the house and kitchen cheerful with great fires befitting Christmas eve, I prepared to sit down . . ." (**p.95**).

b) "I set him a stool by the fire, and offered him a quantity of good things; but he was sick and could eat little, and my attempts to entertain him were thrown away." (**p.101**).

In passage a) Nelly is making the house warm and welcoming for Christmas, and in passage b) she is trying to include Heathcliff in those festivities, but here the image is associated also with Heathcliff's emotions and his inability to express or give vent to them. He is preoccupied with "trying to settle how I shall pay Hindley back. I don't care how long I wait."

c) "The master told me to light a fire in the many-weeks deserted parlour, and to set an easy-chair in the sunshine by the window." (**p.172**).

Here the fire is intended to warm and to cheer the invalid Catherine, who has been remembering nostalgically and longingly the soft thaw wind and warm sunshine of the Heights. She does not respond to it for a while, "enjoying the genial heat", but she soon becomes "greatly exhausted" again. Notice how the fire at the Grange cannot do for her what she believes "the soft thaw wind and warm sunshine" of Wuthering Heights could. We remember how, shut in her room, when "'utter blackness overwhelmed me'", she describes to Nelly how "'the whole last seven years of my life grew a blank! I did not recall that they had been at all. I was a child; my father was just buried, and my misery arose from the separation that Hindley had ordered between me and Heathcliff . . . supposing at twelve years old, I had been wrenched from the Heights, and every early association, and my all in all, as Heathcliff was at that time, and been converted at a stroke into Mrs Linton, the lady of Thrushcross Grange, and the wife of a stranger; an exile, and outcast, thenceforth, from what had been my world – You may fancy a glimpse of the abyss where I grovelled!'" The fire cannot help Catherine, but "'I wish I were out of doors – I wish I were a girl again, half savage, and hardy, and free . . . I'm sure I should be myself were I once among the heather on those hills. Open the window again wide, fasten it open!'" (**p.163**). Emily Brontë leaves us in no doubt as to the main cause of Catherine's illness, as she sees it: exile from the world to which she really belongs and which she shares with Heathcliff.

d) "'No, I don't wish to go upstairs,' he said. 'Come in, and kindle *me* a fire, and do anything there is to do about the room.'" (**p.362**).

Nelly is describing the day before Heathcliff's death. This passage follows a description of Heathcliff talking to Catherine and "spoken as one would speak to a person present – low and earnest, and wrung from the depth of his soul." The fire suggests the immense build-up of emotion in Heathcliff, as he approaches the moment for which he has waited – his ultimate union with Catherine in death.

There is more direct metaphorical use of fire in the novel. On **page 121**, Catherine tells Nelly that Heathcliff's soul, like hers, is made of fire, and on **page 135** Nelly describes his eyes as "full of black fire".

Notes:

Water:

Water images in *Wuthering Heights* take several forms: snow, rain, streams and tears. Like the other elemental images, they are common and significant. They form part of the wider 'storm' images, like the images of air.

SUGGESTED REFERENCES:

a) Lockwood "arrived at Heathcliff's garden gate just in time to escape the first feathery flakes of a snow shower." (**p.51**).

Here we see Wuthering Heights associated with storm and hostile elements – like the air "cold as impalpable ice".

b) Nelly and Cathy go for a walk "On an afternoon in October, or the beginning of November – a fresh watery afternoon, when the turf and paths were rustling with moist withered leaves, and the cold, blue sky was half hidden by clouds, dark grey streamers, rapidly mounting from the west, and boding abundant rain – I requested my young lady to forego her ramble because I was certain of showers." (**p.262**).

In this passage the "boding rain" reflects Cathy's mood: "She went sadly on: there was no running or bounding now, though the chill wind might well have tempted her to a race."

c) "'It is not my fault that I cannot eat or rest . . . you might as well bid a man struggling in the water rest within arms-length of the shore! I must reach it first and then I'll rest.'" (**pp.362, 363**).

The metaphor of the struggling man conveys forcefully the primitive, elemental nature of his passion: Catherine is, indeed, his life – as necessary to him as breathing.

d) Hareton, on the night of Heathcliff's death, "sat by the corpse all night, weeping in bitter earnest" (**p.365**); and he digs Heathcliff's grave "with a streaming face."

The tears Hareton sheds over Heathcliff suggest both the depth of his feelings and his own generous and forgiving nature.

Notes:

WINDOWS (Q.4).

All the window images in the novel suggest barriers, which separate characters from each other and from their hopes or desires.

SUGGESTED REFERENCES:

a) The most striking window image in the novel is in Ch.3, where Lockwood attempts to stop the rubbing of the branch against his window and encounters the "spectre" of Catherine. (**pp.66, 67**).

Lockwood's dream or visitation indicates his fear of the elemental passions loose in Wuthering Heights (he has already told us of his reluctance to commit himself to "a most fascinating creature, a real goddess, in my eyes, as long as she took no notice of me." **p.48**) – he must shut them out at any price. And, of course, for Heathcliff the visitation is exactly what he has longed for ever since Catherine died and which is denied him.

b) Heathcliff and Catherine look through the drawing-room window of Thrushcross Grange at Edgar and Isabella Linton. (**p.89**).

Here we see the separate worlds of the moors and Thruscross Grange on different sides of the window. Catherine is attracted, and will eventually be seduced, by the world within; so it is fitting that she should be taken in and looked after by the family, while Heathcliff is seen as the vagabond, thieving gipsy who threatens 'civilised' society, and he is rejected. The window here starts by separating Heathcliff and Catherine from Edgar and Isabella, but it ends by uniting Catherine and the Lintons inside the house, with Heathcliff alone outside.

c) Nelly leaves the window open for Heathcliff to visit Catherine's open coffin (**p.204**).

In this passage, we see Nelly enabling Heathcliff to cross the barriers which have separated him and Catherine in life. There have been a number of other window images in the pages leading up to Catherine's death, in which we see her in her "seat in the window", (**p.184**) looking out towards the moors or sitting "in the recess of an open window" (**p.192**), waiting for Heathcliff's last visit. He promises her, "'. . . if I live, I'll see you again before you are asleep. I won't stray five yards from your window.'" (**p.198**).

d) When Nelly and Cathy are imprisoned in Wuthering Heights, they look frantically for a means of escape: "We tried the kitchen door, but that was fastened outside; we looked at the windows – they were too narrow for even

Cathy's little figure." (**p.303**). On page **316** we learn that Cathy finally makes her escape – symbolically – through her mother's window.

e) Nelly observes "the master's window swinging open, and the rain driving straight in." (**p.364**).

Here Nelly is describing finding Heathcliff's body lying on his bed, the window open and the rain "driving straight in". She goes on to say, "The lattice, flapping to and fro, had grazed one hand that rested on the sill; no blood trickled from the broken skin, and when I put my fingers to it, I could doubt no more – he was dead and stark!" In death, Heathcliff is one with the elements to which he belongs; the window is open between him and the moors, the wind and the rain. The image recalls, of course, that early visitation of the child Catherine to Lockwood, but Heathcliff is now beyond jealousy or envy.

Notes:

GATES AND DOORS (Q.5).

The images of gates and doors serve very much the same purpose as windows in the novel. Shut, they represent barriers between people; open, they suggest barriers removed. The image is introduced on the first page of *Wuthering Heights*.

SUGGESTED REFERENCES:

a) When Lockwood first arrives at Wuthering Heights, Heathcliff 'greets' him with "walk in!"' "The 'walk in' was uttered with closed teeth, and expressed the sentiment, 'Go to the Deuce'; even the gate over which he leant manifested no sympathising movement to the words . . . When he saw my horse's breast fairly pushing the barrier, he did pull out his hand to unchain it . . ." (**p.45**).

This scene establishes right at the beginning of the novel barriers which Heathcliff has erected against intrusion from the outside world.

b) Catherine locks herself into her room, barring it against both Nelly and Edgar (**p.157**).

This passage follows the scene where she has locked Edgar, Heathcliff and herself into the kitchen, in an attempt to stop servants coming to Edgar's help in 'throwing out' Heathcliff. The image here suggests her emotional separation from Edgar, whom she blames for not accepting Heathcliff's place in her life.

c) "When he [Mr Kenneth] came, and I requested admittance and tried to open the door, I found it locked; and Heathcliff bid us be damned." (**p.364**).

This passage is just before the account of Heathcliff's death. He has locked his door against the intrusion of anyone as he goes to his union with Catherine. The open window (See Question 4e) emphasises where he belongs.

d) "I had neither to climb the gate, nor to knock – it yielded to my hand . . . Both doors and lattices were open." (**p.338**).

This is the scene which greets Lockwood when he returns to the Heights at the end of the novel. It is in marked contrast to the opening of *Wuthering Heights*. By now, Catherine and Hareton are in love and the barriers that separated Earnshaws and Lintons are removed.

Notes:

ANIMAL IMAGERY (Q.6).

Most of the animal images in the novel – and there are a great many – suggest the aggressive, violent nature of the characters they describe. Where the images are not aggressive ones, they are there to suggest weakness or helplessness.

SUGGESTED REFERENCES:

a) The names of the dogs at Wuthering Heights – Gnasher, Wolf and Throttler – suggest the violent nature of the place.

b) In Chapter 10 Catherine describes Heathcliff as "a fierce, pitiless, wolfish man" who would "'crush you, like a sparrow's egg, Isabella.'" (**p.141**). And Nelly tells Isabella, "Banish him from your thoughts, Miss . . . He's a bird of bad omen." (**p.142**).

c) Catherine says to Isabella, "'There's a tigress . . . hide your vixen face! How foolish to reveal those talons to *him*.'" (**p.145**).

d) On page **153**, Heathcliff says of Edgar, "'Cathy, this lamb of yours threatens like a bull! . . . It is in danger of splitting its skull against my knuckles.'"

e) And Catherine joins Heathcliff's attack on Edgar with, "'Heathcliff would as soon lift a finger at you as the king would march his army against a colony of mice'" (**p.154**) and, in the same passage,

f) "'Your type is not a lamb, it's a sucking leveret.'"

Notes:

HELL, FIEND, DEVIL (Q.7).

There are repeated references in the novel to these terms, usually in relation to Heathcliff, but used elsewhere as well. The cumulative effect of them is to suggest the rejection of traditional Christian values which Wuthering Heights – and Heathcliff in particular – represents.

SUGGESTED REFERENCES:

a) Nelly and Joseph talk of a conventional 'Christian' hell: a place of punishment for sinners. For both Catherine and Heathcliff separation from each other constitutes the only hell they acknowledge. In Chapter 15 Heathcliff says to Catherine, "'. . . you know that I could as soon forget you as my existence! Is it not sufficient for your infernal selfishness, that while you are at peace I shall writhe in the torments of hell?'" And Catherine replies, "'. . . I only wish us never to be parted – and . . . think I feel the same distress underground.'" (**p.196**).

When Nelly urges Heathcliff to send for some minister to show him how unfit he will be for heaven, "Unless a change takes place before you die", Heathcliff replies, ". . . you remind me of the manner that I desire to be buried in . . . No minister need come; nor need anything be said over me. I tell you, I have nearly attained *my* heaven; and that of others is altogether unvalued and uncoveted by me!" Nelly is "shocked at his godless indifference", but he perseveres with his point, "'I believe you think me a fiend!' he said, 'something too horrible to live under a decent roof!'". (**pp.363, 364**)

This passage at the end of the novel reinforces what we have seen throughout *Wuthering Heights*: As Catherine rejected heaven in her dream, so Heathcliff wants no part of Nelly's traditional Christian hopes for his soul.

And Joseph's comment at his death concludes the scene and the image: "'The' divil's harried off his soul. Ech! what a wicked un he looks girning at death!'". (**p.365**).

b) In Chapter 3 Lockwood refers to Cathcrine at his window as "the little fiend" and "wicked little soul". (**p.69**).

c) Heathcliff has "an almost diabolical sneer on his face" (**p.55**) and Nelly accuses him of "the most diabolical deed that ever you did" when Catherine is dying and Edgar on his way to the room (**p.199**).

d) Heathcliff, in turn, challenges Edgar with, "'Unless you be a fiend, help her first – then you shall speak to me!'" (**p.199**).

e) In Chapter 14 Heathcliff says of Catherine, "'Oh, I've no doubt she's in hell amongst you . . . You talk of her mind being unsettled. How the devil could it be otherwise, in her frightful isolation?"' (**p.190**).

f) When Isabella escapes from the Heights and tells her story to Nelly, she refers to Heathcliff's "devilish nature" and to "his kin beneath" (**p.209**) and describes his forehead as "diabolical" (**p.215**).

g) Hareton, who has learnt his language from Heathcliff, says to Cathy, "'Will you go to the devil! . . . and let me be!'" (**p.343**).

h) Heathcliff calls the younger Catherine "witch", (**p.319**) and "Damnable witch!" (**p.350**). And she herself taunts Joseph with, "I've progressed in the Black Art" (**p.57**). Such 'art' she has learned at Wuthering Heights under Heathcliff's tutelage.

There are many other examples we could include here, particularly characters swearing by or telling others to go to the devil. Heathcliff and Hindley, as well as Hareton (See Question 7g), frequently use these images.

Notes:

BOOKS (Q.8).

Books are a recurring image in the novel. Many of the images are simply literal references to reading, the main leisure pastime of the period and of the Brontës themselves; but there are suggestions, too, that books are associated sometimes with power, sometimes with freedom and self-realisation.

SUGGESTED REFERENCES:

a) Nelly says, "'I have read more than you would fancy, Mr Lockwood. You could not open a book in this library that I have not looked into, and got something out of also, unless it be that range of Greek and Latin, and that of French – and those I know one from another: it is as much as you can expect of a poor man's daughter.'" (**p.103**).

Nelly's superior education – albeit self-acquired – gives her a powerful position in the household, where she has become, if not the equal of her employers, the trusted confidante.

b) Cathy bribes one of the grooms with "books and pictures" to deliver her and Linton's letters (**p.279**).

Clearly here the books buy freedom from the restraints imposed by Edgar and Nelly.

c) Linton and Cathy share a common interest in books – she brings him "some of my nicest books" and reads to him (**p.282**), and he boasts that he will inherit everything at the Grange, "All her nice books are mine" (**p.312**).

Here the books suggest the power which Cathy has lost and Linton has gained by their marriage.

d) Cathy says of her books, "'I was always reading when I had them . . . and Mr Heathcliff never reads; so he took it into his head to destroy my books.'" (**pp.331, 332**).

Heathcliff rightly sees Cathy's books as a symbol of her refusal to submit to him and an attraction to Hareton, whom he has brought up illiterate to avenge himself on Hindley. But Heathcliff's destruction of all her books fails to reduce Cathy to the servitude he intends for her. Although Hareton, goaded by her teasing, hurled his secret collection of books on the fire (**p.333**), it is his desire for learning and Cathy's willingness to teach him to read which finally brings them together and renders Heathcliff's power over them ineffective.

e) "Both doors and lattices were open," Lockwood tells us when he comes upon the two at their lesson. "The male speaker began to read. He was a young man, respectably dressed, and seated at a table, having a book before him. His handsome features glowed with pleasure, and his eyes kept impatiently wandering from the page to a small white hand over his shoulder . . ." (p.338).

It is through this image that we see the final uniting of the Linton and Earnshaw families.

There are many other references to books in the novel: Joseph has his "Blessed Book", the Bible; Edgar takes refuge in his library, "shut . . . up among books that he never opened" after Cathy has shut herself in her room in response to his demand that she stop seeing Heathcliff. Cathy pretends to read a book while hiding from Nelly and Edgar her letters to or from Linton, and Nelly "got a book and pretended to read" when she was spying on Cathy (**p.267**). Books, in several of these examples, are clearly associated with pretence, a 'cover' for other activities.

Notes:

IMAGES CATHERINE ASSOCIATES WITH HEATHCLIFF AND EDGAR (Q.9).

HEATHCLIFF:

When Catherine tells Nelly why she has "'no more business to marry Edgar than I have to be in heaven'", she goes on to say, "'whatever our souls are made of, his [Heathcliff's] and mine are the same, and Linton's is as different as a moonbeam from lightning, or frost from fire.'" (**p.121**). She and Heathcliff belong to lightning and fire and earth – the moors – rather than to heaven. Later in the same conversation she tells Nelly, "'My love for Linton is like the foliage in the woods. Time will change it, I'm well aware, as winter changes the trees. My love for Heathcliff resembles the eternal rocks beneath – a source of little visible delight, but necessary.'"

24

EDGAR:

In the passage above, we see Edgar associated with "moonbeam" and "frost" and "foliage" which changes with the seasons. In Chapter 11 Catherine attacks him with, "'Your cold blood cannot be worked into a fever; your veins are full of ice-water, but mine are boiling, and the sight of such chilliness makes them dance.'" (**p.156**). Edgar, then, is seen by Catherine as belonging to quite different elements from those to which she and Heathcliff belong, and the imagery thus serves to reinforce Heathcliff's and Catherine's union and the separateness of Edgar and Catherine. He belongs to the "cold"; she and Heathcliff to the heat of passion. Their rightful world is the moors, not the heaven to which Edgar, as a good Christian, aspires. Their spirits will be seen, at the end of the novel, wandering the moors.

In addition to these images, Edgar is also described by Catherine as "a sucking leveret" (**p.154**) – her scorn is scathing.

Notes:

THRUSHCROSS GRANGE AND WUTHERING HEIGHTS (Q.10).

There are very obvious ways in which the two houses are contrasted; their physical situations, for instance, are quite different. Thrushcross Grange is in a sheltered valley, surrounded by parkland; Wuthering Heights is high on the moors, exposed to the winds and rain. But the contrasts go much deeper than this, as David Cecil pointed out in *Early Victorian Novelists*, published in 1934: "The setting is a microcosm of the universal scheme as Emily Brontë conceived it. On the one hand, we have Wuthering Heights, the land of storm high on the barren moorland, naked to the shock of the elements, the natural home of the Earnshaw family, fiery, untamed children of the storm. On the other, sheltered in the leafy valley below, stands Thrushcross Grange, the appropriate home of the children of calm, the gentle, passive, timid Lintons. Together each group, following its own nature in its own sphere, combines to compose a cosmic harmony. It is the destruction and re-establishment of this harmony which is the theme of the story."

Yet the first picture we have of Thrushcross Grange is not one of calm. Heathcliff tells Nelly, "'– ah! it was beautiful – a splendid place carpeted with crimson, and crimson-covered chairs and tables, and a pure white ceiling bordered by gold, a shower of glass-drops hanging in silver chains from the centre, and shimmering with little soft tapers.'" And in the midst of this splendour – compare the description of Wuthering Heights in the opening chapter of the novel – "'Isabella . . . lay screaming at the farther end of the room, shrieking as if witches were running red hot needles into her. Edgar stood on the hearth weeping silently, and in the middle of the table sat a little dog shaking its paw and yelping, which, from their mutual accusations, we understood they had nearly pulled in two between them. The idiots! . . . I'd not exchange, for a thousand lives, my condition here for Edgar Linton's at Thruschross Grange.'" **(p.89)**.

There is contrast here certainly, but is it a contrast between calm and storm? As the novel progresses, we become aware of other contrasts: between 'civilised' and 'uncivilised' behaviour, between 'culture' and 'nature'; between the conventional, 'Christian' passive world of Thrushcross Grange and the elemental, passionate, 'pagan' world of Wuthering Heights.

Notes:

ISOLATION (Q.11).

GEOGRAPHICAL ISOLATION:

We see this particularly in the setting of Wuthering Heights itself, but Thrush-cross Grange is also isolated – note the references to how far Cathy has to ride and her ignorance of the surrounding countryside and hamlets; and also Lockwood's going round in circles even after he reaches the park boundaries in the snow (**p.73**). There is no 'sense' of other people being anywhere in the near vicinity of either house.

SPIRITUAL AND EMOTIONAL ISOLATION
OF THE CHARACTERS:

Most of the characters in the novel are spiritually or emotionally isolated. For a time, Hindley and Frances escape that isolation, but, after Frances' death, Hindley is plunged back into his solitary world. Catherine and Isabella are isolated because they choose partners who belong to different 'spheres' from their natural ones; and Heathcliff is isolated because of Catherine's choice of Edgar as husband. The young Cathy is kept deliberately physically isolated from external influences by her father because of his fear of Heathcliff, and she is further isolated when she is married to Linton and living at the Heights with Heathcliff. For much of the novel, Hareton is in a state of complete emotional isolation, subjected, as he is, to Heathcliff's determination for revenge on Hindley. (We cannot forget, though, that Hareton becomes and remains deeply attached to Heathcliff, however unfulfilling that relationship might be.) Only at the end, with Cathy's and Hareton's love, is there a suggestion that the potential for physical, spiritual and emotional union is likely to be realised.

It is impossible to consider this theme of isolation without looking at the much more complex nature of Catherine's and Heathcliff's love for each other. There is a sense, of course, in which the kind of union they represent is more complete, more whole than any human 'marriage' or earthly union can provide; but their tragedy is, also, of course, that they themselves frustrate the possibilities which their natures possess, hence the unbearable bitterness of their remorse and mutual castigation. Like all Shakespeare's tragic heroes, they are responsible for their own downfall. Unlike them, however, they go to their deaths in the firm hope of eternal union.

VENGEANCE (Q.12).

The desire for vengeance centres mainly on Heathcliff: he seeks revenge on Hindley for his harsh treatment of him in his youth but prinicipally because he ascribes to him the loss of Catherine: "'I'm trying to settle how I shall pay Hindley back. I don't care how long I wait, if I can only do it, at last. I hope he will not die before I do!'" (**p.101**). To 'pay Hindley back', he not only manipulates him into parting with Wuthering Heights and making Hindley himself dependent on him (Heathcliff); but he also brings up Hindley's son as a social outcast, denying himself and Hareton the natural affection which they feel for each other. As Heathcliff tells Nelly "'. . . he's no fool; and I can sympathise with all his feelings, having felt them myself. I know what he suffers now, for instance, exactly . . . I've got him faster than his scoundrel of a father secured me, and lower; for he takes a pride in his brutishness. I've taught him to scorn everything extra-animal as silly and weak. Don't you think Hindley would be proud of his son, if he could see him? almost as proud as I am of mine. But there's the difference; one is gold put to the use of paving stones, and the other is tin polished to ape a service of silver. Mine has nothing valuable about it.'" (**pp.252, 253**). And at the end of the novel, he says, "'Five minutes ago, Hareton seemed a personification of my youth . . . his startling likeness to Catherine connected him fearfully with her . . . Well, Hareton's aspect was the ghost of my immortal love, of my wild endeavours to hold my right, my degradation, my pride, my happiness, and my anguish –'" (**pp.353, 354**).

It is not just in relation to Hindley, though, that Heathcliff seeks vengeance. He marries Isabella to avenge himself on Edgar for marrying Catherine, and for the same reason he insists on bringing up Linton himself – a process which is a continual act of vengeance, sadistically inflicting on the boy fear and torment. His scheming to marry the younger Catherine to Linton is part of his vengeful plan against Edgar, as is his subsequent ill-treatment of her.

But it is not only Heathcliff who seeks revenge. Both Hindley and Isabella express their desire for vengeance on Heathcliff. Hindley's resentment goes back to his childhood, when he felt that his father favoured Heathcliff. At the end of Chapter 4, the two boys quarrel over the couple of colts Mr Earnshaw has given them. Heathcliff threatens, "'I'll tell how you boasted that you would turn me out of doors as soon as he dies, and see whether he will not turn you out directly.'" – to which Hindley makes the impotent response, "'Take my colt, gipsy, then! . . . And pray that he may break your neck; take him, and be damned, you beggarly interloper! and wheedle my father out of all he has, only afterwards show him what you are, imp of Satan! . . .'" (**p.80**).

And later, we hear how Hindley has "a curiously constructed pistol, having a double-edged knife attached to the barrel. 'That's a great tempter to a desperate man, is it not? I cannot resist going up with this, every night, and trying his door. If once I find it open, he's done for! . . . Am I to lose *all*, without a chance of retrieval? Is Hareton to be a beggar? Oh, damnation! I *will* have it back; and I'll have *his* gold too; and then his blood; and hell shall have his soul! It will be ten times blacker with that guest than ever it was before!'" (**p.177**).

While Isabella would like vengeance for Heathcliff's treatment of her, she shows a moral awareness of the dangers of retribution, as befits a 'Christian' Linton: "'I'm weary of enduring now . . . and I'd be glad of a retaliation that wouldn't recoil on myself; but treachery and violence are spears pointed at both ends – they wound those who resort to them, worse than their enemies.'" (**p.211**). We remember Macbeth's fear "that we but teach/ Bloody instructions, which, being taught, return/ To plague th'inventor: this even-handed justice/ Commends th'ingredients of our poisioned chalice/ To our own lips." (*Macbeth* I, vii, 8-12). Whether the 'poison' comes from within or without is really immaterial here.

Notes:

SYMPATHY FOR HEATHCLIFF (Q.13).

There are various ways in which Emily Brontë engages our sympathy for Heathcliff. Firstly, he is an abandoned orphan; then, after Mr Earnshaw's death, he is Hindley's victim, degraded and excluded from the life of the rest of the family. On page **94** we learn from Nelly, "Nobody but I even did him the kindness to call him a dirty boy, and bid him wash himself, once a week . . ."

Even when we are most critical of Heathcliff ourselves, Emily Brontë ensures our sympathy by reminding us of his suffering. In Chapter 29 she describes how Heathcliff orders Cathy back to Wuthering Heights to join Linton after her father's death. He is brutal and sadistic here; but the passage is followed by Heathcliff's description to Nelly of how he got the sexton to remove the lid of Catherine's coffin so that he could see her face; and he goes on to talk about how she has haunted him all these years "incessantly – remorselessly – till yesternight." (**p.320**).

But the most important way in which Emily Brontë establishes her sympathy for Heathcliff is by giving him and Catherine, when speaking of or to him, the most passionate language in the novel. It is this language which engages the emotions of the reader. We find such passages where Catherine is explaining to Nelly why she cannot marry him (Chapter 9), when she talks of not being able to rest until Heathcliff is with her (Chapter 12), when Heathcliff describes his love for Catherine compared to Linton's (Chapter 14), in the last scene between Catherine and Heathcliff (Chapter 15), in the next chapter describing Heathcliff's reaction to Catherine's death; and, of course, in the final scenes of the novel when Heathcliff recalls the days following Catherine's death and describes his suffering since then. The language used is that of high passion: "'do not leave me in this abyss, where I cannot find you! Oh, God! it is unutterable! I *cannot* live without my life! I *cannot* live without my soul!'" (**p.204**). It is punctuated with exclamation and repetition and with highly charged words like "life", "soul" and "unutterable". It has an urgency about it, conveyed by the short, breathless sentences.

Notes:

THE 'UNION' OF CATHERINE AND HEATHCLIFF (Q.14).

In Chapter 9, when Catherine is telling Nelly how she has no business to marry Edgar, she says, "'. . . if the wicked man [Hindley] in there had not brought Heathcliff so low, I shouldn't have thought of it. It would degrade me to marry Heathcliff now, so he shall never know how I love him; and that, not because he's handsome, Nelly, but because he's more myself than I am . . .'" (**p.121**). And later, in the same conversation, she explains, "'. . . surely you and everybody have a notion that there is, or should be, an existence of yours beyond you. What were the use of my creation if I were entirely contained here? My great miseries in this world have been Heathcliff's miseries, and I watched and felt each from the beginning; my great thought in living is himself. If all else perished, and *he* remained, I should still continue to be; and, if all else remained, and he were annihilated, the Universe would turn to a mighty stranger. I should not seem a part of it . . . Nelly, I *am* Heathcliff – he's always, always in my mind – not as a pleasure, any more than I am always a pleasure to myself – but as my own being . . .'" (**p.122**).

In Chapter 15, the whole burden of Heathcliff's desperate outcry against Catherine is, "'Why did you betray your own heart, Cathy? . . . You loved me – then what *right* had you to leave me? What right – answer me – for the poor fancy you felt for Linton? Because misery, and degradation, and death, and nothing that God or Satan could inflict would have parted us, *you*, of your own will, did it . . . What kind of living will it be when you – oh, God! would *you* like to live with your soul in the grave?'" (**pp.197, 198**).

And, after her death, he calls on her, (note the use of her maiden name), "'Catherine Earnshaw, may you not rest, as long as I am living! You said I killed you – haunt me, then! . . . Be with me always – take any form – drive me mad! only do not leave me in this abyss, where I cannot find you! Oh, God, it is unutterable! I *cannot* live without my life! I *cannot* live without my soul!'" (**p.204** – See also the previous question).

In Chapter 33, Heathcliff tells Nelly, "'I have a single wish, and my whole being and faculties are yearning to attain it. They have yearned towards it so long, and so unwaveringly, that I'm convinced it *will* be reached – and *soon* – because it has devoured my existence . . .'" (**p.354**). His one wish is, of course, to be reunited with Catherine in death. He has already described to Nelly, in Chapter 29, his bribing of the sexton to remove the side panels of his and Catherine's coffins when he is finally laid beside her.

What both Catherine and Heathcliff *say* about their relationship is that they are

31

one inseparable being, and that neither is complete without the other. The language they use is the language of the religious mystic, the language of poetry. It is marked by exclamation, repetition, dashes indicating breathlessness, excitement, passion. The vocabulary is often on a grand scale: words like "life", "soul", "Universe", "God or Satan", "annihilated", "existence" proliferate. The imagery (See Question 9) supports their view of their relationship: they belong to lightning and fire, to the moors. The passages which convey most strongly this union are also the most marked in their use of elemental images (See also Question 3).

Notes:

CHARACTERIZATION (Q.15).

HEATHCLIFF:

He is *passionate* (See Questions 9 and 14 for examples); *sadistic* – in his treatment of Isabella, of her dog and of Linton and Cathy; *vengeful* – in his attitude to Hindley, his treatment of Hareton and of Cathy, and in his marriage to Isabella; *loyal* – though, also, of course, obsessional – to Catherine and her memory.

CATHERINE:

She is *passionate* (See Questions 9 and 14 for examples); *hysterical* (see Chapters 11 and 12) – "She rung the bell till it broke with a twang: I entered leisurely. It was enough to try the temper of a saint, such senseless, wicked rages! There she lay dashing her head against the arm of the sofa, and grinding her teeth, so that you might fancy she would crash them to splinters!" **(p.156)**; *concerned about her social status* – she rejects Heathcliff because it would 'degrade' her to marry him; *loyal* – like Heathcliff, she remains loyal to their love, although she has betrayed him by marrying Edgar; *self-centred* – she does not really think about what effect her marriage to Edgar will have on Heathcliff, nor does she recognise the threat he poses to Edgar.

HINDLEY:

He is *capable of love/affection* – in his relationship with Frances; *lacking self-discipline* – in his drinking and gambling after her death, and in his treatment of Hareton; *vengeful* – in his attitude to and treatment of Heathcliff after his father's death; *violent* – seen as a child with Heathcliff and in his later, helpless days.

EDGAR:

He is *gentle* (and/or weak?) – faced with Heathcliff and his bond with Catherine, Edgar gives in, both before and after marriage; *a loving husband and father* – he looks after Catherine to the best of his ability, and he nurtures their daughter protectively; *loyal* – to the memory of Catherine: the day of her death is kept as a sombre occasion every year (despite its being, also, his daughter's birthday) and he spends summer evenings lying on Catherine's grave **(p.289)**; *conventionally(?) religious* – he attends church; he says he would rather "'resign her to God, and lay her in the earth before me'" than leave Cathy in the hands of Linton and Heathcliff **(p.289)**.

CATHY:

She is *strong-willed*, seen in her determination to continue her relationship with Linton and in her dealings with Heathcliff; *affectionate/loving* – to her father, Linton and Hareton; *sensitive* – to her father's illness and to Linton's distress; and she has a *strong survival instinct*, seen in her attitude to Heathcliff's treatment of her. She is determined to survive her imprisonment at the Heights and his cruelty.

33

LINTON:

He is *timorous and cowed*, seen in the way he cringes before Heathcliff and is terrified of disobeying him; *self-pitying* – his own position is so appalling that he finds it impossible to sympathize with anybody else's; he is *dishonest and deceiving* in that he tricks Catherine into going to the Heights, because Heathcliff has ordered him to do so (Chapter 27); he is also, of course, *in great need of affection and care* – his desperate need is seen in the way he manipulates Catherine into staying with him and looking after him (Chapters 23 and 27).

HARETON:

He is *sensitive*, but his harsh upbringing has made him "rude and surly"; he *feels inadequate socially* – he tells Cathy, "'Nay! you'll be ashamed of me every day of your life . . . And the more, the more you know me, and I cannot bide it!" (**p.345**); he is *loyal to Heathcliff*, whom he loves as a father. Nelly reports how he tells Cathy, "If he were the devil, it didn't signify; he would stand by him; and he'd rather she would abuse herself, as she used to, than begin on Mr Heathcliff." (**p.351**). At Heathcliff's death, "Hareton sat by the corpse all night, weeping in bitter earnest. He pressed its hand, and kissed the sarcastic, savage face that every one else shrank from contemplating; and bemoaned him with that strong grief which sprang naturally from *a generous heart*, though it be *tough as tempered steel*." (**p. 365**). As this passage and his love for Cathy shows, he is *capable of deep emotion*.

LOCKWOOD:

He is a *perceptive observer* – note the detail of his descriptions; he is *vain* and assumes women will find him attractive; he is *reluctant to commit himself emotionally*, as we see from his own account of the woman from whom he "at every glance retired colder and farther" (**p.48**); he is *sensitive to the mood of people and place*: "In winter, nothing more dreary, in summer, nothing more divine, than those glens shut in by hills, and those bluff, bold swells of heath." (**p.336**). We have seen this quality already in the early scenes at Wuthering Heights – the way in which he conveys the violent, pent-up emotions of the characters and place, and his account of Catherine's visit at the window. (See also Question 17a.)

NELLY DEAN:

Nelly is *warm and approachable* – many of the characters in the novel confide in her (Catherine, Heathcliff, Cathy, Isabella, for instance); she is *self-educated* – "'I have undergone sharp discipline which has taught me wisdom; and then, I have read more than you would fancy, Mr Lockwood. You could not open a book in this library that I have not looked into, and got something out of also, unless it be that range of Greek and Latin, and that of French – and those I know one from another: it is as much as you can expect of a poor man's daughter.'" (**p.103**). She is also *self-righteous*: she 'lectures' a number of the other characters on the nature of their duty – "'You are aware, Mr Heathcliff . . . that from the time you were thirteen years old, you have lived a selfish, unchristian life; and probably hardly had a Bible in your hands during all that period . . .'" (**p.363**), and of Catherine she says, "I blamed her, as she deserved, for bringing it all on herself" (**p.184**). To Cathy she says, "'I'm dreadfully grieved at you, Miss Cathy, you've done extremely wrong . . . you are a cunning little fox, and nobody will put faith in you any more.'" (**p.228**). Nelly is also *interfering, self-important, hypocritical*, as we see throughout the novel. She also has a *remarkable memory for events, dates and conversations*. (See also Question 17b.)

Notes:

EMILY BRONTË'S NARRATIVE METHOD (Q.16).

Although there are only two obvious narrators, Lockwood and Nelly Dean, many of the characters in the novel tell their own story, either as narrative or through dialogue. The reader experiences their emotions and thoughts directly: exact conversations are quoted verbatim, sometimes at great length. Nelly is either a participant in these conversations or a silent bystander/reporter, whose comments in relating the narrative may or may not influence the reader. Lockwood, as first narrator, presents the outer frame of the narrative, bringing to it his perception and eye for detail and his awareness of the world outside the Heights and the Grange. He – compare Nelly's role (See Question 17b) – provides a detached account; but the 'inner narratives' (where, for instance, Catherine and Heathcliff speak for themselves with passionate intensity) are what 'carry' the reader, involve him or her in the story.

The double-narrator method facilitates the moving back and forth in time, also, since Lockwood belongs to the present and Nelly spans the whole period of the novel: in her retelling of the story and his experience of Heathcliff in the present, there is obvious scope for weaving and inter-weaving of the narrative. (See also Question 18.)

Notes:

LOCKWOOD AND NELLY AS NARRATORS (Q.17).

LOCKWOOD:

Lockwood is the outsider, coming into a world which he finds hostile and bewildering. He is a city gentleman, who stumbles on a primitive 'uncivilised' world which he does not understand, but which fascinates him.

His reluctance to commit himself in love and his mild, vain interest in Cathy contrast with Heathcliff's complete and passionate commitment to her mother.

Because he brings his own conventional attitudes to people and situations, Lockwood misreads what he finds at Wuthering Heights: Cathy is Heathcliff's "amiable lady" (**p.55**); then – when Heathcliff puts him right – perhaps she is Hareton's wife (**p.55**); even the dead rabbits he mistakes for live kittens (**p.52**).

But Lockwood – with all his limitations – is intelligent and perceptive; and his precise, detailed descriptions are used by his creator to convey subtle changes in situations and in character. Lockwood comments, for instance, on the chained gate when he first arrives at the Heights (**p.45**); at the end of the novel, when he returns to find Heathcliff dead, "Both doors and lattices were open" (**p.338**). And it is through his eyes that we see the change in both Cathy and Hareton: "the little witch" (**p.57**) has "a voice, as sweet as a silver bell" (**p.338**) and "the clown" and "boor" of the opening pages (**p.55**) has become "a young man, respectably dressed" with "handsome features" (**p.338**).

Lockwood, then, by fulfilling the role of the detached outsider and observer is able to bring a dimension to the novel which is quite different from Nelly's contribution.

NELLY:

Charlotte Brontë, in her Preface to the 1850 edition of *Wuthering Heights*, made what may now seem to us an extraordinary statement about Nelly: "For a specimen of true benevolence and homely fidelity, look at the character of Nelly Dean" (**p.39**).

She does, of course, manifest these qualities in her loyalty and concern for the Earnshaw family, but her role in the novel is much more complex than this simple description suggests. Is it perhaps her author's ambivalence to Catherine and Heathcliff that she reflects? In contrast to Lockwood, Nelly is wholly involved in her story – she is, indeed, a character within it; and this involvement causes her certain problems.

37

Certainly she treads a difficult path between romantic indulgence and moral rectitude. She both encourages and discourages relationships, appearing to both approve and disapprove of them according to her mood or whim. She arranges that last meeting between Heathcliff and Catherine, for instance, leaving the window open for him to say goodbye to her; yet she has made moral judgements on them, colluding in a situation which brings on Catherine's nervous 'hysterics' and then taking Edgar's part, "'There's nothing in the world the matter,' I whispered." (**p.157**) She plays the same role later in the novel when she both colludes with and judges/betrays Cathy for writing clandestinely to Linton against her father's wishes. In short, she often appears to 'run with the hare and hunt with the hounds' – this ambivalence and her meddling nature often infuriate the reader, who finds her moral stance inconsistent, and even hypocritical.

Nevertheless, she is a vigorous, lively narrator, with a formidable memory. She draws the reader into her story and the lives of her characters by her own energy and her unflagging interest in their stories, and by her detailed recounting of events and dialogue.

Notes:

THE STRUCTURE OF *WUTHERING HEIGHTS* (*Q.18*).

As in Conrad's *Heart of Darkness*, we have in *Wuthering Heights*, two narrators, providing an outer and an inner 'frame'. Lockwood presents us with the outer frame: Wuthering Heights and Thrushcross Grange as they are 'today'. All the major characters of the first part of the novel except Heathcliff – Hindley, Catherine and Edgar – are dead. The present belongs to Heathcliff, Hareton and Cathy, and it is into their world that Lockwood comes in the winter of 1801. Nelly, his housekeeper, provides the inner frame: the story of the Earnshaws and Catherine's and Heathcliff's relationship, her marriage to Edgar and subsequent events. As with Marlow, in *Heart of Darkness*, we see this world through Nelly's eyes, though much of the dialogue is that of the characters themselves, remembered and recorded minutely by Nelly.

As a narrator reporting the past from the present, Nelly is able to depart from straight chronological narrative – she can hint at the future, as in this passage when she says of Heathcliff, "He complained so seldom, indeed, of such stirs as these, that I really thought him not vindictive – I was deceived completely, as you will hear." (**p.81**). And, speaking of the infant Linton, she reports Heathcliff as saying, "'But I'll have it . . . when I want it. They may reckon on that!' Fortunately, its mother died before the time arrived, some thirteen years after the decease of Catherine, when Linton was twelve, or a little more." (**p.218**).

So we have in *Wuthering Heights* Lockwood's diary account, spanning the period from December 1801 to September 1802, in which he tells the reader what Nelly tells him about the families of Wuthering Heights and Thrushcross Grange; and the structure dictates the movement from present to past to future to present which marks the novel. This movement in time is sometimes confusing on first reading, but the chronology is actually very precise and clear, as we see in U.C. Knoepflmacher's table and A. Stuart Daley's correction of Sanger's chronology.

Knoepflmacher's table indicates the relationship between Lockwood/Nelly time (December 1801-September 1802) and Catherine/Heathcliff time (summer 1771-January 1803). Heathcliff , of course, is present throughout the whole time span of the novel, except for the last eight months.

THE INTERNAL CHRONOLOGY OF WUTHERING HEIGHTS

Reproduced with permission from Cambridge University Press, Shaftesbury Road, Cambridge, UK – U.C. Knoepflmacher; Emily Brontë – Wuthering Heights. Landmarks of World Literature series 1989, pp.xviii-xx (ISBN 0-521-31244-2 PB).

Chapter	Lockwood/Nelly time	Catherine/Heathcliff time
4	Early December 1801: Nelly's narrative at Grange.	Summer 1771: Heathcliff brought to Heights at age 7(?); meets Hindley (14), Nelly (14), and Catherine (6).
5,6		October 1777: Old Earnshaw dies; Hindley returns with Frances.
3	Late Nov. 1801: Lockwood reads diary, dreams, leaves Heights.	November 1777: Catherine/Heathcliff defy Hindley and Joseph.
6	Dec. 1801: Nelly's story.	Third week, Nov. 1777: Catherine detained at Grange; Heathcliff returns to Heights.
7	break in story	Christmas Eve and Day, 1777: Catherine returns; Lintons visit Heights.
8	story resumed	June 1778: Hareton born; late 78: Frances dies.
9	story stopped	Summer 1780: Catherine tells Nelly she will marry Edgar; Heathcliff leaves; Catherine catches fever. Autumn 1780: Elder Lintons are infected and die. April 1783: Catherine marries Edgar.
10	Late December 1801 (4 weeks after); Heathcliff visits Lockwood at Grange; Nelly resumes story on same day.	September 1783: Heathcliff returns.

Chapter	Lockwood/Nelly time	Catherine/Heathcliff time
11		December 1783: Nelly meets Hareton.
12		10 January 1784: Catherine's delirium, Isabella elopes (2 a.m.).
13, 14	Story interrupted by doctor's visit	13 March 1784: Isabella and Heathcliff return to Heights; 15 March: Nelly visits.
15	Nelly resumes story "at different sittings" (December 1801-January 1802).	19 March 1784: Catherine and Heathcliff part in violent farewell.
16		20 March 1784: Catherine dies after giving birth to Cathy; 24 March: her funeral.
[29], 17		24-25 March: Heathcliff excavates grave; nearly kills Hindley; attacks Isabella, who runs away. September 1784: Linton Heathcliff born; Hindley dies.
18		June 1797: Cathy meets Hareton at Penistone Crags.
19, 20		June 1797: Isabella dies; Edgar brings Linton back, but allows Heathcliff to take him to the Heights.
21		March 1800: Nelly and Cathy taken to Heights to see Linton.
22		Autumn 1800: Heathcliff tells Cathy that Linton Heathcliff is ill.

Chapter	Lockwood/Nelly time	Catherine/Heathcliff time
23, 24		November 1800: Nelly is ill for three weeks; Cathy meets Linton.
25	Nelly stops and resumes story	June 1801: Edgar declines.
26, 27	Story continues	August 1801: Nelly and Cathy go see Linton and are kidnapped a week later; Cathy and Linton marry (Monday).
28		August or September 1801: Nelly is released; Cathy escapes; Edgar dies before altering his will.
29		September 1801: Heathcliff takes Cathy away from Grange.
30	Mid-January 1802: Nelly finishes her story; Lockwood decides to leave.	October 1801: Linton Heathcliff dies; Hareton tries to please Cathy.
1	[6-7 weeks earlier in time]	Late November 1801: Heathcliff receives visit from his tenant at the Grange, a Mr Lockwood.
2, 3		Early December 1801: Lockwood visits Heights a second time, stays overnight, sleeps in Catherine's bed, screams, is taken back to Grange by Heathcliff.
31	Mid-January 1802 ——————Mid-January 1802: Heathcliff is informed by Lockwood that his tenant is vacating the Grange.	

Chapter	Lockwood/Nelly time	Catherine/Heathcliff time
32	September 1802: Lockwood visits Grange, finds Nelly at Heights; she brings him up to date.	February 1802: Nelly moves to Heights. March 1802: Hareton has an accident; Cathy befriends him.
33		March/April 1802: Cathy defies Heathcliff; Heathcliff's behaviour changes.
34	September 1802: Nelly ends her second narrative; Lockwood visits graves.	May 1802: Heathcliff stops eating; Heathcliff dies. 1 January 1803: projected wedding of Cathy and Hareton.

A. Stuart Daley shows the chronology, in detail, of the events in the novel from Hindley's birth in 1757 to Cathy's and Hareton's marriage in 1803.

A CHRONOLOGY OF WUTHERING HEIGHTS

Reprinted with the permission of the Henry E. Huntington Library.

This chronology both amplifies and silently corrects the 1926 chronology by C. P. Sanger. As I have explained in "The Moons and Almanacs of *Wuthering Heights*", the novel years 1784 and 1802 conform to the Easter, weekdays, and ephemeris of the calendar for 1826, and the novel years 1800 and 1801 conform to 1827. The source of calculation is the more than six hundred temporal allusions in the novel. Some day-dates may, however, be qualified as "on or about". Critics have placed Heathcliff's death variously between April and, even, June. But the reasons for taking April 15 as the latest possibility appear in my "The Date of Heathcliff's Death: April, 1802", *Brontë Society Transactions* 17 (1976): 15-17. The 1826 and 1827 "Almanack for Yorkshire, Durham, Northumberland, Westmorland, and Cumberland" were consulted for astronomical data and special days, e.g. the Quarter Sessions in West Riding.

Year	Season/Month/Day	Event (by Chapter)
1757	Before September	Hindley Earnshaw born
1762	Before September	Edgar Linton born
c.1764		Heathcliff born

43

Year	Season/Month/Day	Event (by Chapter)
1765	Summer	Catherine Earnshaw born
1765	Late in year	Isabella Linton born (6, 10)
1771	September, start of harvest	Mr Earnshaw brings Heathcliff home (4)
1773	Spring/early summer	Mrs Earnshaw dies (4)
1774	October	Hindley Earnshaw sent to college (5)
1777	Before mid-September	Hindley Earnshaw marries (5)
1777	An October evening	Mr Earnshaw dies (5); Hindley is master of the Heights (6)
1777	Sunday, November 19	Catherine and Heathcliff rebel against Sabbath discipline (3); they are caught intruding at Thrushcross (6)
1777	Sunday, December 24	Catherine returns from Thrushcross (7)
1777	Monday, December 25	Earnshaws visit the Heights; Heathcliff excluded from the Christmas party (7)
1778	June, start of haying	Hareton Earnshaw born; later in year or in early 1779, Frances Earnshaw dies
1780	Two days in early summer, full moon	Major episode, beginning with Edgar Linton's visit, climaxed by Heathcliff's disappearance, and ending with Catherine's coming down with a fever (8-9)
1780	Autumn	Catherine convalesces at Thrushcross; senior Lintons catch her infection and die (9)
1783	Spring or early summer	Edgar and Catherine marry; Ellen joins Catherine at Thrushcross (9)
1783	Thursday, September 11, Harvest moon	Heathcliff returns (10)
1783	October	Isabella in love with Heathcliff (Edgar at Quarter Sessions sitting of October 24) (10)
1783	December/early January 1784	Ellen sees Hareton; Heathcliff kisses Isabella (11)
1784	Monday, January 9, Plough Monday	Quarrel between Edgar and Heathcliff; Catherine locks herself in bedroom, refuses to eat (11)
1784	Friday, January 13	Catherine delirious; at 2 a.m. Isabella elopes with Heathcliff (12)
1784	Monday, March 13	The Heathcliffs return to the Heights (13)

Year	Season/Month/Day	Event (by Chapter)
1784	Wednesday, March 15	Ellen brings letter from the Heights to Catherine (11)
1784	Sunday, March 19, Palm Sunday	Heathcliff visits Catherine; passionate leave-taking (15)
1784	Monday, March 20	Catherine II born about midnight; 2 a.m. her mother dies (16, date given in 21)
1784	Tuesday, March 21 Vernal Equinox	Heathcliff puts lock of his hair in Catherine's locket (16)
1784	Friday, March 24 Good Friday	Catherine is buried (16); Hindley's attempts to kill Heathcliff (17)
1784	Saturday, March 25 Lady Day	Isabella runs away (17)
1784	September	Linton Heathcliff born about eight months after his parents elope (17, 19)
1784	September	Hindley Earnshaw dies; Heathcliff acquires Heights (17, 19)
1797	July	Cathy Linton meets Hareton, who shows her around Penistone Crags (18)
1797	Beginning of August	Edgar brings Linton Heathcliff home following Isabella's death; Heathcliff takes Linton to Heights (19, 20)
1800	March 20	Cathy Linton and Ellen meet Hareton and go to the Heights to see Linton Heathcliff; Edgar forbids Cathy's correspondence with Linton (21)
1800	Tuesday, October 30	Heathcliff induces Cathy to visit Linton at Heights (22)
1800	Wednesday, October 31, Almanack for 1827 forecasts "cold with rain"	Cathy and Ellen visit Linton; Ellen ill after getting wet (23)
1800	Thursday and Friday, November 1 and 2	Cathy disobeys Edgar and sees Linton at Heights (29)
1800	Saturday, November 3 Full Moon	Hareton reads in moonlight the inscription above Heights entrance (29)
1800	Wednesday, November 21	Ellen leaves her sickroom (24)
1800	Sunday, November 25 First Quarter moon, 6 p.m.	Ellen surprises Cathy returning from Heights at about 9 p.m. (24)

Year	Season/Month/Day	Event (by Chapter)
1801	February-June	Edgar in failing health (25)
1801	March 20	Edgar too ill to keep remembrance vigil at Catherine's grave (25)
1801	Thursday, August 23	Cathy and Ellen meet Linton (26)
1801	Thursday, August 30	They meet again; Heathcliff confines Cathy and Ellen to Heights (27)
1801	Friday, August 31	Marriage of Cathy and Linton (27)
1801	Tuesday, September 4	Ellen released, returns to Thrushcross to find Edgar dying (28)
1801	Wednesday, September 5, Harvest Moon	Cathy escapes, reaches Thrushcross at 3 a.m; Edgar dies before sunrise, intestate (28)
1801	September "evening after the funeral"	Heathcliff takes Cathy to Heights (29)
1801	Autumn	Linton Heathcliff dies; Hareton friendly to Cathy (30)
1801	October 10, old Michaelmas, observed as a quarter day	Lockwood rents Thrushcross
1801	November	Lockwood calls at Heights (1)
1801	November, next day	Lockwood calls again, is snowbound, spends night at Heights (2, 3)
1801	November, next day	Lockwood takes ill and Ellen Dean begins her story (4)
1801	December, about the tenth and three weeks later	Heathcliff sends Lockwood the last grouse of the season (10)
1801	December, one week	Heathcliff calls (10)
1802	January, one week later	Lockwood continues Ellen's tale (15)
1802	January, second week	Before leaving next week, Lockwood calls at Heights (31)
1802	Beginning of February	Ellen moves to Heights (32)
1802	Early March	Hareton housebound after hunting accident (32)
1802	Monday, March 27 Easter Monday cattle fair at Haworth	Cathy kisses Hareton (32)
1802	Tuesday, March 28	Heathcliff experiences "a strange change approaching" (33)

Year	Season/Month/Day	Event (by Chapter)
1802	Beginning of April	Heathcliff "swallows nothing for four days" (34)
1802	Before April 15 (for week of tenth, forecast for "Windy, with rain or sleet")	Heathcliff dies on windy, rainy night and is buried beside Catherine (34)
1802	Saturday, September 16, Splendid Harvest Moon	Lockwood returns and Ellen updates story; concluding scene in light of full moon (32-34)
1802	October 9, Michaelmas Quarter Day Eve	Last day of Lockwood's tenure of Thrushcross
1803	January 1	Cathy and Hareton to marry (34)

STYLE (Q.19).

There are four obvious 'styles' in *Wuthering Heights*: the one used by Lockwood, Nelly's, that which distinguishes the passionate speech of Catherine and Heathcliff, and Joseph's Yorkshire dialect.

LOCKWOOD'S NARRATIVE STYLE:

Lockwood uses an educated, literary language, marked by detailed factual description and perceptive observation and comment, both on situation and character – as we see in this description of Hareton, "Meanwhile, the young man had slung onto his person a decidedly shabby upper garment, and, erecting himself before the blaze, looked down on me from the corner of his eyes, for all the world as if there were some mortal feud unavenged beween us. I began to doubt whether he were a servant or not . . . his bearing was free, almost haughty, and he showed none of a domestic's assiduity in attending on the lady of the house." (**pp.53,54**).

Sentences are often complex, consisting of a number of clauses, or long phrases, frequently separated by dashes or semi-colons: "He – probably swayed by prudential considerations of the folly of offending a good tenant – relaxed a little, in the laconic style of chipping off his pronouns and auxiliary verbs, and introduced what he supposed would be a subject of interest to me . . ." (**pp.49,50**). Note the self-consciousness of the language and the use of words of latin origin. We find an example of a more complex style at the end of Chapter 3:

"My human fixture and her satellites rushed to welcome me; exclaiming, tumultuously, they had completely given me up; everybody conjectured that I perished last night; and they were wondering how they must set about the search for my remains.

I bid them be quiet, now that they saw me returned, and, benumbed to my very heart, I dragged upstairs, whence, after putting on dry clothes, and pacing to and fro, thirty or forty minutes, to restore the animal heat, I am adjourned to my study, feeble as a kitten, almost too much so to enjoy the cheerful fire and smoking coffee which the servant has prepared for my refreshment." (**p.73**).

Note the number of adjectival and adverbial phrases, enclosed by commas: "Benumbed to my very heart", "after putting on dry clothes", "to restore the animal heat", "feeble as a kitten". While some serve simply to provide additional information, others are used metaphorically or to reinforce a point through visual image. The length and complexity of sentence structure indicate a narrator whose command of language is sophisticated.

NELLY'S NARRATIVE STYLE:

Much of Nelly's story consists of dialogue related verbatim and, as such, is not her language at all, but that of the major characters in *Wuthering Heights*. When she is speaking as narrator, her language is colloquial, lively and imaginative: "'Rich, sir!' she returned. 'He has nobody knows what money, and every year it increases. Yes, yes, he's rich enough to live in a finer house than this, but he's very near – close-handed; and, if he had meant to flit to Thrushcross Grange, as soon as he heard of a good tenant he could not have borne to miss the chance of getting a few hundreds more.'" (**p.75**).

The repeated "yes, yes" and words and phrases like "close-handed", "flit" and "could not have borne" bring Heathcliff to life with their immediacy. We recognize this language as that of everyday, colloquial speech. Later, in the same passage, she says of Heathcliff's history, "'It's a cuckoo's, sir – I know all about it, except where he was born, and who were his parents, and how he got his money, at first. And Hareton has been cast out like an unfledged dunnock!'" (**p.76**). The "at first", tagged on, as it is, as an afterthought, attracts our attention – so she does know how he got his money later: our interest is aroused. The bird images convey vividly and precisely Heathcliff's 'history'.

THE PASSAGES OF 'POETIC' PROSE:

See Questions 13 and 14. The passages concerned here are those relating to Catherine's and Heathcliff's relationship, and are 'spoken' by one of them. As pointed out in Question 13, they are to be found particularly in Chapters 9, 12, 14, 15, 29 and in the final chapters of the novel. See Question 14 for character-istics of style in these passages, but, briefly, they are marked by exclamation, repetition, dashes, short sentences, visual 'elemental' imagery, vocabulary on a grand and universal scale. Note also the use of italics (**p.122** and **p.354**, for instance).

THE LANGUAGE OF JOSEPH:

The Yorkshire dialect spoken by Joseph gives a certain natural, realistic authenticity to the setting of the novel, and perhaps reinforces its sense of isolation. Dialect words are to be found used by other characters in the novel, but Joseph's is the only sustained use of it. William Sale, in his Textual Commentary to the Norton (Third) Critical Edition comments that "Emily Brontë seems to have been surprisingly successful in rendering the sounds of the northern dialect, though her method is not always consistently employed" and it is interesting to note that he goes on to say, "Christopher Dean points out that sometimes her spelling suggests a sound not common to the north of England but suggestive of Irish, as when she uses *spake* for *speak*, *clane* for *clean*, *stale* for *steal*, *dacent* for *decent*." We remember that contemporaries commented on Charlotte's Irish accent. In the isolation of the Parsonage – removed as it was from direct outside influence – it would not be surprising if they adopted unconsciously some of the characteristics of the native speech of their father and a succession of Irish curates.

Notes:

HOSTILITY TO *WUTHERING HEIGHTS*
ON PUBLICATION (Q.20).

Many of the contemporary reviews of *Wuthering Heights* make certain points in common:

a) the novel is coarse in its use of language;

b) many of the incidents and characters in the novel are 'brutal' and 'savage';

c) it does not have a recognizable moral purpose.

COARSE LANGUAGE:

". . . If we did not know that this book has been read by thousands of young ladies in the country, we should esteem it our first duty to caution them against it simply on account of the coarseness of the style . . . The whole tone of the style of the book smacks of lowness." (G.W. Peck, *American Review: A Whig Journal of Politics*, June 1848). The writer goes on to say that the book "will live a short and brilliant life, and then die and be forgotten"!

"It may be well also to be sparing of certain oaths and phrases, which do not materially contribute to any character, and are by no means to be reckoned among the evidence of a writer's genius." (*Examiner*, 8 January 1848).

The reviewer in *Literary World*, April 1848, refers to "the disgusting coarseness of much of the dialogue".

E. Whipple, in *North American Review*, October 1848, writes that the author of *Wuthering Heights* "exhausts the whole rhetoric of stupid blasphemy."

And Charlotte Brontë, in the Preface to the 1850 edition of *Wuthering Heights*, feels obliged to defend her sister: "Men and women who, perhaps naturally very calm, and with feelings moderate in degree, and little marked in kind, have been trained from their cradle to observe the utmost evenness of manner and guardedness of language" will find the novel shocking, "and will suffer greatly from the introduction into the pages of this work of words printed with all their letters, which it has become the custom to represent by the initial and final letter only – a blank line filling the interval . . . The practice of hinting by single letters those expletives with which profane and violent persons are wont to garnish their discourse, strikes me as a proceeding which, however well meant, is weak and futile. I cannot tell what good it does – what feeling it spares – what horror it conceals."

BRUTALITY OF INCIDENT AND CHARACTER:

A reviewer writing in *Examiner*, 8 January 1848 says ". . . the people who make up the drama, which is tragic enough in its consequences, are savages ruder than those who lived before the days of Homer . . ."

"The scenes of brutality are unnecessarily long and unnecessarily frequent," writes the reviewer in *Britannia*, 15 January 1848.

"How a human being could have attempted such a book as the present without committing suicide before he had finished a dozen chapters, is a mystery. It is a compound of vulgar depravity and unnatural horrors . . ." (*Graham's Lady's Magazine*, July 1848).

". . . the coarseness extends farther than the mere style; it extends all through . . ." (G.W. Peck, *American Review: A Whig Journal of Politics*, June 1848).

LACK OF RECOGNIZABLE MORAL PURPOSE:

The reviewer of *Spectator*, 18 December 1847 refers to "the moral taint" about the "incidents" in *Wuthering Heights*.

"What may be the moral which the author wishes the reader to deduce from the work it is difficult to say, and we refrain from assigning any, because, to speak honestly, we have discovered none but mere glimpses of hidden morals or secondary meanings. There seems to us great power in this book, but it is a purposeless power, which we feel a great desire to see turned to better account." (*Douglas Jerrold's Weekly Newspaper*, 15 January 1848).

"This novel contains undoubtedly powerful writing, and yet it seems to be thrown away. We want to know the object of a fiction . . ." (*Tait's Edinburgh Magazine*, February 1848).

A brief glance at these excerpts from early reviews of *Wuthering Heights* tells us what Emily Brontë's Victorian readers were looking for in a novel and what they did not find in hers. Principally, they expected it to have a moral theme. Instead, they were faced with a work whose creator was clearly ambivalent about traditional Christian morality: Heathcliff is in love, after all, with another man's wife, and it is his 'union' with Catherine – not her marriage to Edgar – that captures the reader's romantic interest.

If *Jane Eyre* had shocked the readers of the 1840s, how much more so would *Wuthering Heights*. Jane at least had the moral decency to go away from Rochester when she found he was married; Heathcliff, on the contrary, flies in the face of all propriety, holding Catherine in his arms in Edgar's house, climbing through a window to say farewell to her and to twine a lock of his hair with hers, and, finally, bribing the sexton to remove the coffin panels that would otherwise separate them in death. Not only is their 'union' adulterous – in spirit if not in fact; but, in traditional Christian terms, it is also idolatrous, since for them heaven is eternal union with each other, not with God.

In addition to this morally reprehensible relationship, Emily Brontë created in Heathcliff a character who openly declares his rejection of the Church; and who, through the imagery and language of the novel, is associated with Hell and the Devil.

It is also true, however, that many of her early readers responded, as we do today, to the sheer power of the novel. As one reviewer put it, "We strongly recommend all our readers who love novelty [!] to get this story, for we can promise them that they have never read anything like it before." (*Douglas Jerrold's Weekly Newspaper*, 15 January 1848).

Notes: